FEB - 3 2020

by Kevin Blake

Consultant: Marjorie Faulstich Orellana, PhD
Professor of Urban Schooling
University of California, Los Angeles

PUBLISHING

New York, New York

Credits

Cover, © aldomurillo/iStock and © cge2010/Shutterstock; TOC, © Byvalet/Shutterstock; 4, © Espiegle/iStock; 5L, © Ekaterina Pokrovsky/Shutterstock; 5R, © Cannon Photography LLC/Alamy; 7, © holgs/iStock; 8L, © kavram/Shutterstock; 8R, © David Ionut/Shutterstock; 9, © michelepautasso/Shutterstock; 10L, © erlucho/Shutterstock; 10–11, © Adwo/Shutterstock; 12, © mcjeff/Shutterstock; 13 (T to B), © JeremyRichards/iStock, © edurivero/iStock, and © Giedriius/Shutterstock; 14, © Album/Metropolitan Museum of Art/Newscom; 15, © Marcelo Vildosola Garrigo/Dreamstime; 16, © Classic Vision/AGE Fotostock; 17, © Jose Luis Saavedra/Newscom; 18L, © Gubin Yuri/Shutterstock; 18–19, © holgs/iStock; 20, © Andrey_Fokin/Shutterstock; 21, © Ruslana Iurchenko/Shutterstock; 22, © reisegraf/iStock; 23T, © Anton Velikzhanin/Alamy; 23BL, © monticello/Shutterstock; 23BR, © kubais/Shutterstock; 24–25, © Xinhua/Alamy; 25T, © CP DC Press/Shutterstock; 25B, © Pablo Rogat/Shutterstock; 26L, © El Mercurio de Chile/Newscom; 26–27, © ampueroleonardo/iStock; 28, © abriendomundo/iStock; 29, © Olga Danylenko/Shutterstock; 30T, © Anton_Ivanov/Shutterstock and © Andrey Lobachev/Shutterstock; 30B, © Warehouse of Images/Shutterstock; 31 (T to B), © Jose L. Stephens/Shutterstock, © Alexandru Nika/Shutterstock, © Ekaterina Pokrovsky/Shutterstock, © KoBoZaa/Shutterstock, © Jeremy Richards/Alamy, and © wanderluster/iStock; 32, © neftali/Shutterstock.

Publisher: Kenn Goin
Senior Editor: Joyce Tavolacci
Creative Director: Spencer Brinker
Design: Debrah Kaiser
Photo Researcher: Thomas Persano

Library of Congress Cataloging-in-Publication Data

Names: Blake, Kevin, 1978– author.
Title: Chile / by Kevin Blake.
Description: New York, New York : Bearport Publishing, [2020] | Series: Countries we come from | Includes bibliographical references and index.
Identifiers: LCCN 2019010063 (print) | LCCN 2019012020 (ebook) | ISBN 9781642805802 (ebook) | ISBN 9781642805260 (library)
Subjects: LCSH: Chile—Juvenile literature.
Classification: LCC F3058.5 (ebook) | LCC F3058.5 .B53 2020 (print) | DDC 983—dc23
LC record available at https://lccn.loc.gov/2019010063

For more information, write to Bearport Publishing Company, Inc., 45 West 21st Street, Suite 3B, New York, New York 10010. Printed in the United States of America.

10 9 8 7 6 5 4 3 2 1

Contents

AMAZING

Surprising

FUN

Chile (CHIL-ee) is a long, narrow country in South America. It stretches 2,650 miles (4,265 km)! It's located along the Pacific Ocean.

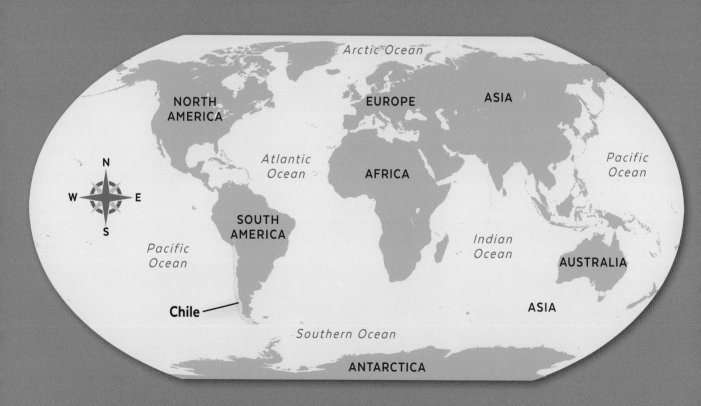

Almost 18 million people live in Chile.

8

Forests and farmland cover other parts of the country.

Chile is known for its rich farmland.

grapevines

One of the driest deserts in the world is in Chile.

It's called the Atacama Desert.

It rains less than 0.5 inches (1.3 cm) per year there!

The desert is rich in minerals, such as copper and iron. Big trucks haul the minerals.

Chile is home to amazing animals.

Llamas eat grass in the hills.

Condors soar in the sky.

Pumas hunt for food.

Penguins live in southern Chile near the ocean.

Chile has a long history.

People settled there over 10,000 years ago!

For many years, the Incas and Mapuche (mah-poo-CHEE) ruled the land.

The Mapuche fought the Incas.

The Ona and Yahgan peoples also lived in Chile at the time of the Mapuche.

Incan artifact

14

a Mapuche-style hut

Ruka umawtuwe

In the 1500s, the Spanish took control of Chile.

On February 2, 1818, Chile gained its **independence** from Spain.

In 1973, a cruel leader took over Chile.

He was defeated in 1988.

Today, Chile is a peaceful **democracy**.

Chileans vote for their leaders.

The **capital** of Chile is Santiago.

It's also the country's largest city.

More than six million people live there.

Valparaíso is the second-largest city in Chile. It's located on the coast.

Chile's main language is Spanish.

This is how you say *good morning* in Spanish:

Buenos dias
(BWAY-nohs DEE-ahs)

This is how you say *horse*:

Caballo
(kah-BAH-yoh)

Some Chileans also speak Quecha, a **native** language.

Yummy! Chilean food is delicious. People love to eat fish from the Pacific Ocean.

Roasted meats are also popular.

Most meals are served with bread or potatoes.

Chilean wine is famous around the world.

What sports do people play in Chile?

Chileans love soccer!

Fans cheer for their national team.

Rodeos and riding horses are also popular in Chile.

The national dance of Chile is called the *cueca* (KWAY-kah).

The dancers hold handkerchiefs.

They twirl around!

Violeta Parra was a famous Chilean folk singer. She's best known for the song "Gracias a la Vida."

Chile has about 5,000 islands.

One is called Easter Island.

There you can find ancient stone figures.

No one knows
exactly how
or why these
wonders were built!

The statues, or
moai (MOH-aye),
weigh up to 14 tons
(13 m tons).

29

Fast Facts

Capital city: Santiago

Population of Chile: Almost 18 million

Main language: Spanish

Money: Chilean peso

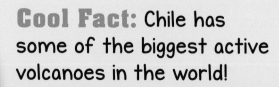

Major religion: Christianity

Neighboring countries: Argentina, Bolivia, and Peru

Cool Fact: Chile has some of the biggest active volcanoes in the world!

capital (KAP-uh-tuhl) the city where a country's government is based

democracy (dem-OK-rah-see) a form of government in which people vote for their leaders

glaciers (GLAY-shurz) huge, slow-moving masses of ice

independence (in-duh-PEN-duhnss) freedom

native (NAY-tiv) original to a place

rodeos (ROW-dee-ohz) contests where cowboys and cowgirls test their horse-riding skills

Index

Read More

Morrison, Marion. *Chile (Countries Around the World).* Portsmouth, NH: Heinemann (2011).

Owings, Lisa. *Chile (Exploring Countries).* Minneapolis, MN: Bellwether (2011).

Learn More Online

To learn more about Chile, visit
www.bearportpublishing.com/CountriesWeComeFrom

About the Author

Kevin Blake lives in Providence, Rhode Island, with his wife, Melissa, his son, Sam, and his daughter, Ilana. He'd love to take a trip to Chile soon!